Life Lines

Shahilla Shariff

LIFE LINES is Shahilla Shariff's first collection of poetry. Drawing on her life experiences, it explores themes of love, grief, dislocation and transition. Her work addresses the vast and unruly dimensions of loss – loss of home, of time, of people, of self – and probes the raw and uncertain trajectory of mourning along with the complex interplay of memory, faith and fate. The poems span continents, generations and cultures, exposing the collisions and contradictions of East and West which underlie her own personal narrative.

SHAHILLA SHARIFF was born in Kenya and is Canadian. A fourth-generation East African, she spent her early childhood in a multi-generational Indian-Muslim household in Dar-es-Salaam. Her family later emigrated to Canada. She was educated at Harvard College, Harvard Law School and Cambridge University, where she was a Commonwealth Scholar. She has been a practising corporate lawyer for over twenty years. She has lived in Hong Kong since 1993.

Proverse Prize Finalist 2011

Life Lines

Shahilla Shariff

Proverse Hong Kong

Life Lines
by Shahilla Shariff, 20 November 2012.

1st published in Hong Kong by Proverse Hong Kong, 20 November 2012.
Copyright © Proverse Hong Kong, 20 November 2012.
ISBN 978-988-19935-7-1

Distribution (Hong Kong and worldwide): The Chinese University Press of Hong Kong, The Chinese University of Hong Kong, Shatin, New Territories, Hong Kong, SAR.
E-mail: cup@cuhk.edu.hk Web site: www.chineseupress.com
Tel: [INT+852] 2946 5300; Fax: [INT+852] 2603-7355
Distribution (United Kingdom): Enquiries and orders to Christine Penney, Stratford-upon-Avon, Warwickshire CV37 6DN, England. Email: <chrisp@proversepublishing.com>
Additional distribution: Proverse Hong Kong, P. O. Box 259, Tung Chung Post Office, Tung Chung, Lantau Island, NT, Hong Kong SAR, China.
E-mail: proverse@netvigator.com Web site: www.proversepublishing.com

The right of Shahilla Shariff to be identified as the author of this work has been asserted by her in accordance with the Copyright, Designs and Patents Act 1988.

Front cover: vintage Gujarati dupatta (private family collection).

Cover design by Artist Hong Kong Company. Page design by Proverse Hong Kong.

Printed in Hong Kong by Artist Hong Kong Company, Unit D3, G/F, Phase 3, Kwun Tong Industrial Centre, 448-458 Kwun Tong Road, Kowloon, Hong Kong.

All rights reserved. No part of this publication may be reproduced, stored in a retrieval system, or transmitted, in any form or by any means, electronic, mechanical, photocopying, recording or otherwise, without the prior written permission of the publisher or publisher and author. The book is sold subject to the condition that it shall not, by way of trade or otherwise, be lent, re-sold, hired out or otherwise circulated without the author's prior written consent in any form of binding or cover other than that in which it is published and without a similar condition including this condition being imposed on the subsequent owner or purchaser. Please contact Proverse Hong Kong (acting as agent for the author) in writing, to request any and all permissions (including but not restricted to republishing, inclusion in anthologies, translation, reading, performance and use as set pieces in examinations and festivals).

Proverse Hong Kong

British Library Cataloguing in Publication Data

Shariff, Shahilla.
Life lines.
1. East and West--Poetry. 2. Loss (Psychology)--Poetry.
I. Title
811.6-dc23

ISBN-13: 9789881993571

for

my sons

and

my mother

∘ *Life Lines*

Introduction

As the day is inevitably fragmented by noise and distraction, I prefer to write at night. The stillness lends itself to stories, and they emerge, finding form in poems. The acoustics of a poem are singular, layered, spreading. Poetry is all about exploration, although we sometimes forget the poetry in exploration itself. For Paul Valéry, a poem was never finished, only abandoned. Where we end is usually somewhere sprawling, with more space for discovery and refinement. We have to stop somewhere. It does not mean we stop reaching.

Life Lines began with an encounter and a gift. A Bedouin from the oasis of El Ain meets a young bride newly arrived in the Gulf. The old veiled woman, now a city-dweller, was almost blind. Over tea and dates in broken Arabic we shared what had brought each of us to this waypoint. As I was leaving, she held me with her heavily hennaed hands and removed the gold ring on her finger, placing it on mine. The ring was stark in its simplicity, etched with the rough lines of a desert palm. It remained on my finger from that day. Only on finishing *Life Lines* did I pull the ring off and put it away in a box. The time seemed right.

These are intensely personal poems. I pause over the ordinary – wrapping a birthday present, waiting at a bus stop for a child, hanging a protective charm over a cradle. Spinning in and out of places, belonging is always a quest. Rootlessness is disruptive but equally, the source of a secret richness – the distinct scent of scattered earth: a nostalgic harking back to my African childhood; the wintry tapestry of a Canadian adolescence; the lasting desolation of an Arabian interlude; the renewal of an Asian inheritance.

Many of these poems began as a meditation on grief. Memories shaped poems; poems shaped memories. A grainy map drew itself, framing the course of a voyage. The central truth: whichever way one looked, loss was everywhere – at different points meaning different things, edging one to live, as Camus urges, "to the point of tears", daring one to love. As much as these poems scream and sing in tune with the specifics of my story, what we have in common is this inescapably huge truth along with its imperative of hope.

In the end, what ignites *Life Lines* is people – lost and found – along with the compulsion to clarify the horror of multiple loss and the persistence of trauma. The endnotes are jarring, but they also intensify the urgency of living. If hope is a condition of revival, then love is the twist in *Life Lines*.

Shahilla Shariff
Hong Kong, October 2012

Table of Contents

Author's Introduction	vii
Punctuating My Life	13
Kuan Yin	14
The Taste of Rain	15
Captive Colours	16
Room With A View	17
Resting	18
Fourteen	19
Maya	20
The New Normal	21
Parting	22
Birdsong	23
Sea of Grief	24
Blue Alchemy	25
Rudraksha	26
Singing My Redemption	27
Residue	28
Lakshmi	29
Job's Tomb	30
New Beginning	31
The Wedge Between	32
Predictions of Snow	33
A Matter of When	34
Later	35
Nostalgia	36
The Sensation of Burning	37
Salalah	38
An Instant in the Wind	40
Orchids	41
Rupture	42
Dumplings	43

Life Lines

Memoir	44
The Way of Things	45
Carry Me Home	46
New Year's Eve	48
Dreamcatcher	49
Love	50
Unwinding Our Beauty	51
Morecambe Bay	52
Clots	53
Metabolism	54
Pilgrim	55
Undersea	56
Wishing Lanterns	58
One Word	59
Isis	60
Raggedy Anne	61
Scent of Green Cardamom	62
Weaving Shrouds	63
Malaika	64
Lakeside	65
At the Bus Stop	66
The Aura of Trees	67
Tea in Hangzhou	68
On the Rue Romain Rolland	69
Signposts	70
Life Lines	71

Life Lines ◦

◦ *Life Lines*

Punctuating My Life

Sally speak to me
your tarot cards never
read your own destiny.

You never anticipated
the seeding overnight
of a tumour tree.

If dying has advanced your powers
send me a spectral sonogram
so I know how to punctuate my life.

Life Lines

Kuan Yin

The maples were burnished that Autumn
we crossed the seas sandwiching
your preciousness between our clothes.
You found your nook – you were there
no matter the season. When I left the girl I was behind,
I touched your face for luck, for fate to be kind.
It was the last time either of us was whole.
My mother said it was our curse that knocked you
off your perch, so what if the real culprit was a clumsy boy.

The kaleidoscopic years in blur.
The rains stopping one day,
the earth rust and damp with random promise,
the anthem of cicadas drawing me onto a path
where truth lay heaving as I stumbled
upon a myriad porcelain goddesses congregating
in a bamboo grove in unbearable iridescence.
Was it you that heard my sound
and restored the silence?

Kuan Yin: roughly translated, "she who hears the sounds of the world"; the goddess of mercy and compassion; seen as a saviour and revered in Buddhism and Taoism and widely throughout East and South East Asia.

The Taste of Rain

My great-grandmother clicks amber prayer beads
on the verandah bench, hand henna tattoos inter-laced
with verdigris veins, kohl-rimmed eyes in wizened face,
holding more secrets than she cares to share.

All the while sun scorched the earth
to resemble burnt pottery;
taste the rain
bouncing off the tin roof.

On my mother's nightstand jasmine withers
to sepia brown in the steam of mid-afternoon;
her history unearthed, time enough
to smoke her letters into banshee winds.

At Kifkoni ferry pier a sea-sprayed moon
hovers in a broken indigo sky, and boys
the colour of night grill silvery fish
mountains over a glowing ember pit.

I freeze the frames,
bury my time capsule along with the old me.
Start the new life of a survivor,
all in an impossibly cold country.

Life Lines

Captive Colours

Walking the sands along a wild Arabian Sea
imagining velvet night of Africa
from the ancestral core, the songs
of wayward dhows a way from home.

Crawling down from Mithapur on a dusty train,
the saffron ecstasy of Dwarka trailing us.
Old Ahmedabad all devotional alcoves,
choked bazaars and storied secrets.

We entered Rani Ka Hazira bared
calloused soles burning against cement
at noon into a hush of marbled coolness
 – a forgotten queen's crypt.

Home now where
I come to shed my skin.
It can be anywhere
as long as we are.

Do not worry
about the perfect place to scatter me.
By then, surely,
I will be found.

Dwarka: a city in Gujarat, regarded as the birthplace of the Hindu god Krishna, and one of the seven holy sites of ancient India.

Room with a View

They soaked your sheets; the stench of bleach
it clung to you as much as the drama of urine, distress.
You were shriveled shrunk to fit their bed.
They refused to unstrap you.
Where would you run?

I fed you cake, sponginess collapsing under
layered chantilly cream, cherry-rich inner-sweet.
My birthday that day the patisserie led to you,
my hand against your wrinkled face,
despair no enigma, both of us left choking.

You knew the highway outside
that window would never take you home,
nor would your cries.
So your eyes, they strayed towards light.
All that was left to contemplate.

Resting

Silence is a sound we seldom hear,
the space between us.
We placed you under a canopy
of verdant leaves, stirring in a breeze
redolent of frangipani, drift of seas.
I am the one left to crumble
in the wait of absence.

Fourteen

Fourteen balloons a marker.
The room so still – you dreaming of presents
I stay awake wrapping past midnight
when I say a prayer, fill the air with quiet blessings
to keep you from harm, to keep you.
The company of ghosts less clamourous
than the jumble of what is living.
Staring at the ceiling,
straining for cracks.
The light, it comes in pieces.

Life Lines

Maya

We remembered your son tonight.
In the wretched abandon of incense,
an unfurling, wet with other dying.

We should have celebrated,
not wailed a wall inside; our harshness
it was unambiguous as the plight of dented stars.

There was no more clemency in ritual.
There was nothing but ash and flare.
We drove back broken: two old people; me.

Is peace a place or a thing?
Is there any point in praying for an easy life,
an easy death being the essential thing?

Maya (Sanskrit): "illusion".

The New Normal

Distance is the new normal.
Why are you here
rubbing against jaggedness
no one can smooth?

We keep churning;
it is the only way we know how,
pausing for mid-afternoon tea, yellowing newspapers,
unfolding incandescence in flame tips of butterflies.

I graze myself – a pottery shard on the beach:
all dull glaze, antique sea green patina.
When I am washed ashore
the world I dream will be new again.

Life Lines

Parting

In another life, someone's wife.
Living for the dead no easy matter
when living itself escapes you.
Love only frees you from so much.
Time and passing, the way we live now.
Somehow or another, sooner or later,
we will be parted.
No there, anywhere.
Here. Only here.

"There is no there there": Gertrude Stein's statement when, on returning to the United States in the 1930s after decades in Europe, she was unable to find her childhood home and other physical reminders of her past.

Birdsong

Some of us get lucky –
the bits that are unglued do not stick
but we grow wings because
somehow flying is in our nature.

○ *Life Lines*

Sea of Grief

I am too sprawling;
I can't be your mother.
I buy a ticket.
I discover there is no end to the world.

Architecture is about escaping.
I loop back to my heart,
its urgent seam of tears,
learn how to deconstruct fear.

I wane into memory, reigning
forever in a happily-ever-after photo montage.
If I could have plugged love,
we would not be swimming in a sea of grief.

Blue Alchemy

Seventy seems like the end
and, in some ways, it is.
You semi-interred, parceling out
bangles, childhood trinkets,
the *mangalsutra* from your wedding chest,
watching your friends leave with no warning
except in dreams that come to you on restive nights.
Prayer more tranquilising than the tumble
of rainbow pills in the bathroom cabinet.
Only your recipes intact.

The roses are opening;
thin bands of light setting
in your father's garden, exploding
with the secret shade of coral
akin to the underbelly
of a conch you once found
where the waves hugged the coast.
The unbound sun, blue alchemy
beckoning now beyond
the sea at your worn feet.

Mangalsutra: a Hindu symbol of a marriage union; a sacred thread which in ornamental terms is normally a variation on a string of black beads.

○ *Life Lines*

Rudraksha

I should return the *rudraksha* beads –
grief after grief is a torrent.
What can rescue me from the feeling
of hope aground somewhere between ashes and dust?
Besides, you need them more.

I saw you pack soup cans into your suitcase last night.
When I end our call will you prepare dinner tonight
in the one room life you have made for yourself?
Lying here, Campbell's soup labels flashing: red; white.
How is this the answer to my prayers?

A husband's days relegated – only so much space for sorrow
in a small brown cardboard box bound for charity.
Still we grow distracted. The wild orchid you left
for dead has bloomed in a corner
where the sun stole in when no one was looking.

Rudraksha (Sanskrit): a seed said to have powerful healing properties. Used as prayer beads and often worn as an amulet; associated with the Hindu god Shiva from whose single tear, legend has it, the rudraksha tree sprang.

Singing My Redemption

You never thought
the time past your womb
would be so fragile.
The karma I'm shaking
is not just my own.
Undo your tears.

I entered kicking, screaming,
never stopping.
Born fighting,
I won't fight dying.
My voice by then will sing
its own redemption.

Residue

I am exorcising the restaurant
opposite the tube stop where you deposited me
in haste that mid-Winter to retreat from the residue
of my takeaway kebabs to order pizza
for small boys last seen in a picture frame.

There are no safety nets in this country
where even my dreams are second-hand.
But the translucence of green jade is compelling
and though your present is cracking,
I continue to wear it.

Lakshmi

Your soul was unadorned
but what good was that to you?
I glimpsed your eyes.
It was a flash,
but there was no denying
the rattle of the divine.
Just then the mahout rapped you
and you bent your trunk
to bless me for one rupee
before moving manacled
to the next devotee
at the steps of your temple.

Mahout: a keeper and rider of elephants.

Job's Tomb

We passed by it I recall.
Now I see the signs but
there is no meaning
in suffering if your life is no parable.
My children's wings are pinned to glass
how can they revel
in the vastness of their reach?

Job: appears in a number of religious traditions, including Islam, where he is regarded as a prophet and a symbol of steadfastness to God despite being tried through intense suffering. His tomb is said to be in Jabal Qara outside the city of Salalah in Southern Oman.

New Beginning

An opal moon fragments,
quickening longing into pulse,
disrupting the filigree
screen of my seclusion.

In Singapore Tiresias lives;
a bird woman of Little India
lifting the bars of her parakeet's cage
to tap havoc, havoc.

I spread myself on a charpoy,
uncurling into the ballad
of a startled minstrel
the permanence of journeys.

And we part the moth-messed gauze
of your monumental curtained bed,
collapsing the frail sky
in a wide new beginning.

We synchronise our dreaming
in the time of spirits cusping
a dawn of crows, and love is an ode
rising above the ruin.

Tiresias: in classical Greek mythology, a blind prophet and soothsayer.
Charpoy: a simple string bed of traditional origin common on the Indian Subcontinent and consisting of knotted ropes stretched over a wooden frame.

Life Lines

The Wedge Between

Tidying day's end, tea leaves
stuck to a glass – solace sought
at four in the afternoon before clocking
again the prospect of home.

Sun escaped me that day
as on so many such days merging
one into the other, mercifully, mercilessly,
I have not decided which.

Make piles, create lists,
organise tasks, check boxes.
There is no way to mitigate
the drastic intensity of our mess.

On a cork bulletin board:
Buddha heads and buildings –
your drawings jostling photographs of us three
so alive you would think we were free.

Predictions of Snow

You ask for a photograph for your album –
you who have never seen snow before.
"Can you bring it home in your pocket?"
No tourists this time why are we so completely lost?
The only miracle is you.
When you measure a life, every bit is fraught.

A tableau vivant of skaters: Rockefeller Center
rigged at Christmas. If we could stop the melting
we would. Heaven such an abstraction.
All I have left for you is the snow globe I found
in the airport arcade. If you shake it hard enough,
you can make the sensation of snow last longer.

Life Lines

A Matter of When

What could have been, should have been, never was.
Another year; another wedding night unremarked.
Votive candles may be taunting
but there is more comfort
in building shrines than in moving on.

Next I will be quilting scraps
of our togetherness to wrap my solitude.
There are no perfect endings,
simply the consolation of climbing dunes,
watching shifting hues in the limitless sky.

Truth in layers is relentless.
You, long gone,
have I think an inkling
beyond the almost imperceptible
stillness of blue flames.

So sorely ravaged
I hang in tatters.
What is inviolate
you and I both know:
loss is a matter of when.

Later

He was not the one you would have chosen
but over time you learned to knead his chapatis
effortlessly, molding them into perfectly formed
discs to resemble the face of the moon.
You were both old when he bought you
that sari you would have craved as a girl:
a diaphanous yellow French chiffon
you chided him for but fragranced with oudh
before tucking away from his sentimentality.
Its loveliness lingered; it reminded him
of so much he said, but mostly of you.
He wondered why you never
draped it over you, why you left it
on a shelf to be anointed by dust.
You could have given it away.
Later, later was what you always said.
You only remembered
when he was no longer there
to make you blush
the contours of your regret.

Chapati: a round flat unleavened Indian bread made of wheat flour; traditionally cooked on a griddle; a staple of many regional cuisines, including of Gujarat. Oudh: a rare perfume resin from agar trees; prized in the Middle East and South Asia; when burnt with charcoal in clay containers, the fumes release a long-lasting fragrance.

Nostalgia

The dress still fits.
I take it out of tissue once a year –
its swan white perfection softly
recalling the places it took me.
I pay it silent homage
although I no longer wear it.

The Sensation of Burning

Ashes would have freed me from so much;
I never shaved my head, abandoned colour
but inside no question of fate.
It was understood. If I had accepted
what was always meant to be,
I would not be searching for fire
in the half-life of my crypt,
where the slightest hint of fallen sunlight
tricks me into the possibility of day.

Salalah

The whole night she prayed;
the bars at the window
casting long shadows about us both –
anonymous burqa-wrapped
she was my stranger, my host.
I curling into the bed
where sleep never came,
clasping my cotton tee-shirt
stiffened as it was by blood stains,
the only familiarity mapping
the raw end to love just
as we arrived at it.
Replaying it all with punishing clarity,
dazed at the exact hour
you hovered unsure whether
to turn back condemned
or fly free, peace so tantalisingly close
now forever ripped like my youth
and that thing even more sacred than it all,
which was the hope that left us brimming.

Morning came.
I could not recognise
who it was in my eyes.
I was mute. I wished I was deaf
and sightless. You in your coffin,
the two of us riding the plane back
side-by-side but only if you grasp the darkness
of an utterly unimaginable journey:

Life Lines

your adopted home, the monochrome green
of an English cemetery at springtime;
my white wedding sari of glistening
Benares silk woven with gold *zari*
so recently concealed in a camphorwood drawer
now restored, never a premonition
of grim reversal, queen of shrouds;
the coarser swaddling that followed,
your naked corpse lowered
down down into the claiming soil,
my brother in his Savile Row suit
pocketing a handful.

Proof so far removed from incantation
in the carpeted quarantine of a distant mosque –
no more is left to weep –
women tearing at their hair
as if that will disintegrate the pain,
leaving me with the memory
of ochre dust rising as we drive
along ancient plains of Sheba
past the *durgahs* of dislodged saints
towards the siren song of possibility,
the emerald lull of the bedazzling sea.

Salalah: coastal capital of the Southern Omani province of Dhofar; known in antiquity and associated with the Queen of Sheba (who supposedly travelled to the region to obtain precious supplies of frankincense) and possibly the site of the tomb of Job. Zari: a type of traditional brocade from the Indian Subcontinent; the thread is composed of gold and silver, lending itself to fine craftsmanship. Durgah: a Sufi shrine usually built over the grave of a revered religious figure or saint.

Life Lines

An Instant in the Wind

There is no pleasure in abiding love –
you disfigure my dreams
in the time you are gone.

Give back Sundays scavenging
the shore with a red plastic bucket
for souvenirs worth keeping.

A starfish disgorged in the foam
that day was the first clue
to the world askew.

Then came a rainbow
to abbreviate the light the instant
our sons trumped the wind swinging.

I would have bitten through chains
to set us free,
but something in me knew the futility.

Orchids

You have gone again.
The room feels crooked,
only the orchids
still rapturous after three days
drenching the air
with your tenderness.

◦ *Life Lines*

Rupture

We were at a cafe
near the Place Vendome when somewhere
between my salade nicoise and your steak frites
something broke.

We almost repaired it that night
you shook me from sleep to your cell phone
crying you wouldn't make it – outside your hotel door,
Lashkar-e-Taiba were drilling through lives.

We were lucky that night;
you grew one life, then two.
I watched your children playing
with my own – that's when it struck me.

Lashkar-e-Taiba (Urdu): "Army of the Good"; one of the largest and most active militant Islamic terrorist groups operating today in South Asia and responsible for the 2008 Mumbai attacks, including at the Oberoi Hotel.

Dumplings

The dumplings are steaming –
I swirl their slippery tautness
into a dipping sauce red with the heat
of Chengdu chilies and eat my way
through a basket of woven simplicity.

Outside by the harbour
at Sai Wan Ho a barge is poised
to float the opaque waves
and berth somewhere known
while I watch unmoored.

◦ *Life Lines*

Memoir

It annihilated us,
evening everything a dismal shade of gray.
The beast still stalks me.
I can't raze its scale, defang its truth.
I interrupt the ceremonial of dust,
the colonising of cobwebs,
your cupboard now belatedly bare.
No discarding the x-rays at the back.
After all there could be rhapsody in grayness,
not in the disappointment and dying,
but in the extraordinary desire
to summon colour, maybe even paint my life back.
I compile a memoir of your malignancy
to showcase in the museum of my memory.
I fabricate its intricacy from tokens.
And now I am truly spent.

The Way of Things

Except in the pattern of tides,
there is no logic, crumpled or otherwise.
It is the way of things.

We squander ourselves in exploration;
the only thing that makes sense
is that there is none.

When I own the truth,
it will no longer distort
the distance between us.

Carry Me Home

Last night I wept an ocean
nobody but an errant star heard.

Before that I memorised your innocence,
the membrane between us bound to be restored.

I have become my own hollowness,
the wind comes skipping through.

Krishna roared his mother to life.
So now we are even, you and I,
climbing the crest in our life-giving boat.

This is the shape of me now:
my breath can cloud a mirror –
please tell me am I living?

There will be good days
I try to remember: I have two of you.

Life Lines ◦

So wish me time
so you can grow tall
so you can paint my portrait
with invisible ink
so you can bid me peace
so a lid can shut
so the earth can open
so I am the gust in your steps
when you carry me home.

Krishna: a central deity in Hinduism. As a child, Krishna opened his mouth in front of Yashoda, his foster mother, to reveal the entire universe. The relationship embodies the pain of separation, particularly with the discovery of Krishna's real parents and identity.

○ *Life Lines*

New Year's Eve

Mumtaz's name
was an emperor's only calling.
You should have known better
than to shut the door behind you:
grief is perfected in singular acts.
I used to think of silence
as an antidote – not a way of life.
Only the present to get through.
What a way to live.
As they come to light the *arti*
on the eve of another year,
see what endures.

Mumtaz: a Mughal Empress and the third and favourite wife of the Emperor Shah Jahan, who built the Taj Mahal as her mausoleum and a testament to his profound and lasting grief after she died giving birth to their fourteenth child. Arti (Sanskrit): a Hindu devotional ceremony symbolic of the central role of divinity in everyday life and involving the ritual lighting of wicks soaked in oil and contained in crude clay pots. Also, short for the *arti* lamp itself.

Dreamcatcher

The dreamcatcher I hung
above your cradle so when you woke
dark would have constricted itself,
leaving the vaguest impression
of gossamer wings, violet anemones
clustered in the gathering light.
You have left me
tangled in tree roots,
watering the earth at your feet
through a veil softly,
forgetting for an instant
the path that winds slowly
into a deeper wood where,
if you stand un-naturally still,
you will find what
I once told you would never die.

Dreamcatcher: a handmade Native American object based on a hoop on which is woven a loose net. It is decorated with sacred charms and hung above the beds of sleeping children to protect them from nightmares; some traditions suggest they alter dreams, allowing good dreams and wonderment to filter through.

Love

When you returned it was the mustiness
in the room you shared that undid you
more than the decay of your circle of plants,
the vacant gaping of the refrigerator,
the sputtering of unchanged light bulbs,
the sight of him sitting at the airport
with a straggle of supermarket flowers,
killing time with an outdated magazine
as he waited in the wrong place.

Unwinding Our Beauty

Princess Margaret died today.
You were a girl in a white dress
and scarlet sash under the umbrella
of a baobab tree the day her sister came
to town and she left a queen crowned
with the posies of my mother-in-waiting.
There was no hint of elegies, only a lush intimacy
in the pigment of pomegranates
dripping like the halo of a dipping sun.

No crystal ball could have foreshadowed
your death the day I cried to expunge
my grief in the river of someone else's dreams.
You unwound our beauty.
You asked for me unborn.
You had no way of buying the boatman;
you willed the winds shift
to sail my pain to a rim so far away
only a lost soul could skim it.

You kneeling could not stop me sinking
so you asked if we could trade lives,
and when this didn't work
you begged for me to grip my faith
so it could ground me,
long enough to watch
your hair turn whiter than the lilies
you wanted me to pick
to label your grave.

Life Lines

Morecambe Bay

You wanted to pick a better life.
I heard about the cockle-gatherers;
a voiceless wave I dreamt
devoured you in moon-less stealth
before you noticed your inability to swim.
You missed our cries,
sequenced our gaps,
forgave yourself inventing
who you wanted me to be.
You lost us both.
When I saw your tears
I was trying to save myself
from drowning in my own pool.

Morecambe Bay: scene of the 2004 tragedy in Northwest England when at least 21 illegal Chinese immigrant workers controlled by gangs were drowned by an incoming tide as they continued collecting cockles.

Clots

I tipped my balance when we said good-bye.
I was an ice floe first
but my beauty was lost in passage.
I was clogged
and when I thawed
I spewed out the ick
in clots
in pools
in giant blobs of stagnant blood.
At least it is out.
But now I am empty
what is the point
of filling myself again?

Metabolism

I am knocking
at the Gate of Life.

No answer.
Herbal litany:
astragalus; schizandra; dong quai.
I decoct their awkwardness,
brew my wellness
but alas no elixir.

Neither is there resurrection
in the cloud comfort of mugwort
after my near-death by needles.
Artemesia Vulgaris rolls off my tongue,
dreams me to sleep. Moxa-seared, I breathe.
Soon, I will start to flow.

Gate of Life: a critical energy point in traditional Chinese medicine associated with the essence of *qi*, the universal life force. *Qi* imbalances, said to result in blockages and illness, are restored using traditional Chinese healing therapies such as herbal remedies, acupuncture and moxibustion.

Pilgrim

There can be no reminiscing
about an unknown me.
I unpack my pilgrim self.
I could live out my days more benignly
but I have found a sharp knife
so I slice time.

Undersea

I should have deciphered our prophecy
in the mythology of our meeting.
Time. Time.
Almost time.
Time for no more time.
Where would you like
your husband to die?
Doctor, doctor,
they anaesthesised your heart
so you could pull mine out
with ungloved hands:
the unexpurgated version
of violently pounded
unashamedly human me.
When were you last exposed
to uncut suffering?
Remove your mask:
watch me roar.

I had an image of you undersea
plunging sun-shot to labyrinth reefs,
limpid other-world depths of magical healing,
not propped up by machines,
subdued by morphine and tragedy.
Our babies were in their downy pyjamas
without anyone to soothe them to sleep.

Life Lines ○

And I yearned for home, as faraway
as the pendulum moon and tinsel stars,
the city winking past your hospital room –
there was life outside, only ours had stalled.
There is no mistaking the stomp of terror in the wake
of accumulated dread. I staked your standard issue bed,
my vigil beginning as you signaled the angel overhead
in the sibilant rasping of your end.
I was teetering. I said let go. Then it was me submerged.
And yours was the soliloquy of the wind
as you lifted into free-fall light.

Life Lines

Wishing Lanterns

Spread a bolt of ebony,
stars pinprick its density.
A village elder's blessing
for paper lanterns uncreased,
wishes we scribble, festoon, release.
They flame past
worn roofs, stone temples, pagoda dots
sprinkled beyond the serpentine inkiness
of a river's edge, against the faraway
ring of bells, itinerant chanting, traffic hum,
receding into midnight's sky
like dreams we wish we could recapture.

Wishing Lanterns: airborne paper lanterns containing a lit candle and often hand-written wishes. They are used in certain Asian countries during celebrations and festivals.

One Word

If only a little white pill could have plugged the pain,
blacked out the blinding glare of another day,
soaked up the aching silence.
The old country full of sacrifice:
a mother's burdens; a daughter's duty
strapped together, handed down –
the secret idiom of generations.
So much to be done when so much is undone.
Will there be time beyond
the brutal rendering of my children's eyes?
Fear is that land with no borders;
the space between remembering
and forgetting a permanent trauma.
Needles in my head. Dislocated *qi*.
Call God. One word.
It should have been enough.

Qi: in Chinese medicine and philosophy, the universal life force or energy responsible for health through a balancing of the complementary and opposing principles of *yin* and *yang*, including through techniques such as acupuncture.

Life Lines

Isis

These are not the kites boys fly
as wind turns to bluster
sky no longer the crucible of calmness.

Dirge-like prayers; prayer-like dirges.
Dying does not unclap our dead
so we struggle with reinvention.

The only constant is inconstancy.
The only way to free a kite
is to tether the night and let it soar.

Isis: ancient Egyptian goddess with a cult following; known as a protector of the dead; often depicted in the bird form of a kite and the harbinger of death and lamentation. She used her magical powers to bring her husband Osiris back to life.

Raggedy Anne

You who sang me past sadnesses
buried beyond the tear-stained brightness
of your doll-face, if only I could reach
for the jingle-jangle madness of your yarn hair.
Now that was a safer time of listening
to voices transport through paper walls,
fault lines laying themselves
grid-like across makeshift worlds –
you pressed tightly against my chest,
another little hand clutching mine,
three of us, co-conspirators in sleepless night,
charting the arc of a single shooting star,
kneeling in prayer, ignoring the static
of a transistor radio, midnight monologues
on Furtwängler's Berlin making exile
infinitely less pronounceable.
All along the snow fell quietly outside.

Wilhelm Furtwängler: a leading early twentieth century German composer and conductor who, for an extended period beginning in 1922, directed the Berlin Philharmonic Orchestra.

Life Lines

Scent of Green Cardamom

Winter's first snow blanketed the world
last night, darkness overrun
by swirly powdery flakes that clung
to the ground for days before
a denouement of watery grey mounds.

Ice winds at the bus stop; I huddle
into a hand-me-down coat, the scent of green cardamom
rising from your new oven. Is it steam from the milky *chai*
you pour into carefully-preserved china cups
that fogs my gaze or my perennially frozen breath?

Chai (Persian): "tea".

Weaving Shrouds

The gardenias of last Summer
dried and pressed are still heady
but you promised to stay not leave me
in the flimsy embrace of solo days,
and I can't trace you by the edges
of footprints in dervish sand.

Nothing takes growing accustomed to.
I weave shrouds. I hold your rawness,
unravel our symmetry, suspend the night.
The veins on my hands are ripening.
We will speak in tongues –
you will know my cadence.

Home you remind me
in postcards is for the world-weary.
I taste the sea settled in the lines
about your eyes, glossy-shiny you
confined to paper. You odyssey
to uncertainty. I fumigate it.

Weaving Shrouds: a reference to the story of Penelope, faithful wife of Odysseus. Numerous suitors, arguing that the long-absent Odysseus was dead, insisted that Penelope choose a second husband from among them. As a delaying tactic, Penelope pretended she had vowed to complete a shroud for her father-in-law before she remarried. She toiled on the shroud every day for three years, only to unravel her work each night.

○ *Life Lines*

Malaika

The last time I saw you
you gave me a betel nut box,
hammered silver, lined
with a mystery wood.
You slipped away
faster than the taste of the jaggery
you hid in my mouth;
you said it would sweeten my life
when I inherited the pungent bitterness
of cloves enfolding your Zanzibar childhood,
the papaya orange Swahili sun staining your heart.

Malaika (Swahili): "angel"; also the name of a timeless and popular song crooned as a lullaby throughout East Africa.

Lakeside

Hold on to faraway sounds of children
long gone. The terrible truth of voices
not carrying. If only the wind would
no longer tug at trees, saturating night,
dimming light, so palpably sad.
Have you noticed the lake's boundary
dissolving into the horizon?
Will you look for me before I too am gone?

At the Bus Stop

The rain fell in sheets today
but when the bus climbed
the hill for once I was waiting
with a battered pink umbrella –
what it felt to be
enfolded in brightness
even if it only lasted
until we crossed the road.

The Aura of Trees

There was something distinctly elegiac in her gait
and in the manner in which she took her place
every afternoon at half past four on the same park bench
to anticipate the sun as it dappled her hands.

She conversed silently with all the birds,
her lament never pronounced but they must have heard.
I think I see her on a branch, those wistful eyes
in a sparrow's face fortified by the aura of trees.

Life Lines

Tea in Hangzhou

When I feared my own fear then I knew
there was no way to rectify the desolation.
I vanquished stairs, voyaged into untamed mists,
rolling clouds: an eroded teahouse beckoned –
melancholy was all around.
The snow billowing into lotuses
collapsing at the edge of the iced lake;
there was nothing to soften the savagery.
So I warmed my hands
on a glass of chrysanthemum tea
and drank the liquid poetry
of hapless petals before sinking.

On the Rue Romain Rolland

What were you thinking
as we walked down the Rue Romain Rolland
past shuttered windows, their paint peeling
in the searing heat of mid-afternoon?
Sister Theresa bent over her embroidery
in the faded colonial grandeur
of a Pondicherry reception room,
no longer conjuring twilight straddling French fields
because home, through force of habit,
or perhaps the prism of authentic love,
was leprosy, starvation, unyielding flies
and any place else was unthinkable.
The dust unsettled, the hour passed
in the whir of countless ceiling fans
until the serving of *masala chai* on a wooden salver
accompanied by two meringues –
at the time it seemed the unlikeliest of pairings.

Masala chai: tea brewed with milk, sugar, and a mix of spices such as cardamom and cloves; popular throughout the Indian sub-continent.

Life Lines

Signposts

Remember the post-it marked 12:45.
Was I meant to stop everything,
pray for you up in heaven?
I think I need the prayers more –
twenty years to the day –
eating leftover dahl
for lunch in a cube,
sun mutilated through glass,
blotches all around me.
We can't contain grief.
We can't finesse death.
We could be part-Chinese:
grasping harmony.
Qu shi, it is said.
You are not dead.
You have left the world
without any signposts
to your frontier.

Qu shi ("qu shi le") (Mandarin Chinese): literally, "to leave the world", a euphemism to skirt the taboo of death.

Life Lines

Into your hennaed hands, my own.
You could not see my face;
you traced the lines on my palm –
Fatima merged in your breath.
So you thought: an amulet
to stave off what was foretold.
An oasis however crudely scratched
on the ring you rushed
from your finger onto mine.
I am not where I started.
I am not yet strangled by winds,
but the lines, they remain fixed.

Fatima: daughter of the Prophet Mohammed and wife of Ali; the object of deep veneration by Muslims. Her suffering occupies a special niche in Shia piety; and the string of prayers offered to her is invested with a particular potency.

Life Lines

FIND OUT MORE ABOUT OUR AUTHORS, BOOKS, EVENTS AND INTERNATIONAL PRIZES

Visit our website
http://www.proversepublishing.com

Visit our distributor's website
<www.chineseupress.com>

Follow us on Twitter
Follow news and conversation: <twitter.com/Proversebooks>
OR
Copy and paste the following to your browser window and follow the instructions: https://twitter.com/#!/ProverseBooks

"Like" us on www.facebook.com/ProversePress

Request our E-Newsletter
Send your request to info@proversepublishing.com.

Availability
Most titles are available in Hong Kong and world-wide
from our Hong Kong-based Distributor,
The Chinese University Press of Hong Kong,
The Chinese University of Hong Kong, Shatin, NT,
Hong Kong SAR, China. Web: chineseupress.com

All titles are available from Proverse Hong Kong
and the Proverse Hong Kong UK-based Distributor.

We have stock-holding retailers in Hong Kong,
Singapore (Select Books),
Canada (Elizabeth Campbell Books),
Principality of Andorra (Llibreria La Puça, La Llibreria).

Orders can be made from bookshops in the UK and elsewhere.

Ebooks
Most of our titles are available also as Ebooks.